# Seminar on the Acquisition
# of Latin American Library Materials

## Bibliography and Reference Series, 36

**Sharon A. Moynahan**
*Executive Secretary*

**Barbara G. Valk**
*Chair, Editorial Board*

# Serial Publications
# Available by Exchange

# Caribbean Area

Compiled and edited by

Shelley Miller
and
Gabriela Sonntag-Grigera

SALALM Secretariat
General Library, University of New Mexico
Albuquerque, New Mexico

## SALALM Sponsoring Member libraries

University of California, Los Angeles
Columbia University
Cornell University
Harvard University
University of Illinois at Urbana-Champaign
University of New Mexico
New York Public Library
Princeton University
University of Southern California
Stanford University
University of Texas at Austin
Yale University

The publication of this volume
was made possible in part
through the support of the

**Latin American Institute
University of New Mexico**

# CONTENTS

# PREFACE

This publication is the second in a series aimed at providing libraries with up-to-date lists of institutions in Latin America currently participating in programs focused on exchanging publications. The first list included institutions in Mexico and Central America and plans are underway for a list of South American institutions. These publications are compiled with the goal of assisting those wishing to acquire materials through exchange agreements. Knowing the names of the institutions and the type of materials they make available through exchange can help in this process. These mutually beneficial programs are at times the only method of acquiring certain publications.

The current list focuses on institutions in the Caribbean area. It provides the institution name and address and the title of the serial publications available for exchange from that institution. The OCLC number for those publications has also been provided to assist in the identification of the publication. The list is arranged alphabetically by country. It is our aim to continue to receive and make available information on the exchange opportunities in this area.

The Caribbean list was a cooperative effort begun by Shelley Miller as Chair of the Gifts and Exchanges Subcommittee of SALALM At the time of Shelley's death in the Spring of 1994 the publication was almost complete. I have updated it with the help of many members of SALALM. It is another example of the cooperative spirit of SALALM.

Gabriela Sonntag-Grigera<br>
San Marcos, California

# CARIBBEAN SERIAL PUBLICATIONS

# Caribbean serial publications

| INSTITUTION AND ADDRESS | PUBLICATIONS AND OCLC NO. |
|---|---|

Department of Information and Broadcasting

Anguilla. Department of Information and Broadcasting. Annual Report

The Valley
ANGUILLA

---

Antigua and Barbuda Chamber of Commerce and Industry Ltd.

Business Expressions — 17741960

Redcliffe St.
P.O. Box 774
St. John's, Antigua
ANTIGUA AND BARBUDA

---

Government Printing Office

The Antigua and Barbuda Official Gazette — 14241889

Statutory Instruments. Antigua and Barbuda

Old Parham Rd.

St. John's, Antigua
ANTIGUA AND BARBUDA

---

Centrale Bank van Aruba

Annual Report. Centrale Bank van Aruba — 23748725

Quarterly Bulletin. Centrale Bank van Aruba — 17014746

Monthly Bulletin. Centrale Bank van Aruba — 17470555

Havenstraat 2

Oranjestad
ARUBA

---

| INSTITUTION AND ADDRESS | PUBLICATIONS AND OCLC NO. |
|---|---|

**Bahamas National Trust Library**

P.O. Box N-4105

Nassau N. Providence
BAHAMAS

| Bahamas Naturalist | |
|---|---|
| | 8810493 |
| Annual Report / Bahamas National Trust | |
| | 10062128 |
| | |
| | |
| | |

**Central Bank of the Bahamas Library**

P.O. Box 4868

Nassau, N.P.
BAHAMAS

| Quarterly Statistical Digest | |
|---|---|
| | 27000910 |
| Quarterly Statistical Review  OR | |
| Quarterly Economic Review | 27000757 |
| Annual Report | |
| | |

**College of the Bahamas Library**

P.O. Box N 4912

Nassau
BAHAMAS

| Cobla Journal | |
|---|---|
| | 29809297 |
| College Forum | |
| | |
| | |
| | |
| | |

**Department of Statistics**

P.O. Box N 3904

Nassau
BAHAMAS

| Vital Statistics Report | |
|---|---|
| | 2855695 |
| Statistical Abstract Report | |
| | 27924315 |
| Bahamas Latest Economic Indicators | |
| | |
| Bahamas Statistical Profile | |

| INSTITUTION AND ADDRESS | PUBLICATIONS AND OCLC NO. |
|---|---|

Department of Statistics

P.O. Box N 3904

Nassau
BAHAMAS

| Annual Review of Prices | |
|---|---|
| | 28607407 |
| Summary Report of Foreign Trade Statistics | |
| | 27332499 |
| Retail Price Index | |
| | 14049162 |
| Social Statistics Report | 9746413 |

Department of Statistics

P.O. Box N 3904

Nassau
BAHAMAS

| Labour Force and Household Income Report | |
|---|---|
| | 20655008 |
| Quarterly Statistical Summary | |
| | 2327217 |
| | |
| | |

Ministry of Agriculture and Fisheries

P.O. Box N-3028

Nassau
BAHAMAS

| Annual Report | |
|---|---|
| | 2486826 |
| | |
| | |

Barbados Development Bank
Library

P.O. Box 50

Wildey, St. Michael
BARBADOS

| Annual Report | |
|---|---|
| | 4451263 |
| | |
| | |

| INSTITUTION AND ADDRESS | PUBLICATIONS AND OCLC NO. |
|---|---|

**Barbados Museum and Historical Society**

St. Ann's Garrison

St. Michael
BARBADOS

| Annual Report | |
|---|---|
| | 20167016 |
| Journal of the Barbados Museum and Historical Society Newsletter | 1519178 |

---

**Barbados Statistical Service Library**

3rd Floor, National Insurance Bldg.
Fairchild Street
Bridgetown
BARBADOS

| Statistical Bulletin:index of retail prices | |
|---|---|
| | 21395984 |
| Digest of Tourism Statistics | |
| | 8091349 |
| Overseas Trade | |
| | 1247664 |

---

**Caribbean Conference of Churches**

P.O. Box 616

Bridgetown
BARBADOS

| Caribbean contact | |
|---|---|
| | 6675716 |
| Christian Action | |
| | 22590315 |

---

**Central Bank of Barbados Library**

P.O. Box 1016

Bridgetown
BARBADOS

| Annual Report | |
|---|---|
| | 20861146 |
| Economic and Financial Statistics | |
| | 3028144 |
| Annual Statistical Digest | |
| | 4119933 |

| INSTITUTION AND ADDRESS | PUBLICATIONS AND OCLC NO. |
|---|---|
| Central Bank of Barbados Library | Balance of Payments of Barbados — 4795881 |
| | Economic Review — 8791564 |
| P.O. Box 1016 Bridgetown BARBADOS | |
| National Library Service | National Bibliography of Barbados — 3838928 |
| Coleridge Street Bridgetown 2 BARBADOS | |
| National Petroleum Corporation | Annual report — 14755162 |
| Wiley St. Bridgetown BARBADOS | |
| Treasury Department Accountant General | Report of the Accountant General — 2239908 |
| | Financial Report of the Accountant General for the month ended... — 24640595 |
| P.O. Box 254 Bridgetown BARBADOS | Accounts and Statements for the month of... — 24640622 |

| | | |
|---|---|---|
| Bermuda Library<br>Par-La-Ville | Report & Accounts of the Consolidated Fund of the Bermuda Government | 21891919 |
| | Report of the Manpower Survey | |
| 13 Queen Street | | 4937711 |
| Hamilton HM 11<br>BERMUDA | | |

| | | |
|---|---|---|
| Bermuda Maritime Museum | Bermuda Maritime Museum Quarterly | 20054169 |
| Box MA 273 | | |
| Mangrove Bay MA BX<br>BERMUDA | | |

| | | |
|---|---|---|
| Bermuda Biological Station for<br>Research, Inc. Library | Annual Report | 14116423 |
| | Contributions from the Bermuda Biological Station for Research | 12963373 |
| Ferry Reach 1-15<br>BERMUDA GEO1 (W.I.) | Currents | 18059376 |

| | | |
|---|---|---|
| Government Information Services | Cayman Islands Annual Report or Cayman Islands | 10157041 |
| 3rd Floor, Tower Bldg., North Church | | |
| Georgetown, Grand Cayman<br>CAYMAN ISLANDS | | |

Legislative Department

| | |
|---|---|
| Hansard Official Report | |
| | 7114684 |

P.O. Box 890

Grand Cayman
CAYMAN ISLANDS

---

Academia de Ciencias de Cuba
Biblioteca Nacional de Ciencia y Técnica

| | |
|---|---|
| Revista Cubana de MedicinaTropical | |
| | 1778854 |
| Revista Cubana de Medicina | |
| | 1778853 |
| Biotecnología Aplicada | |
| | 25477730 |
| Revista Cubana de Medicina Militar | |

Apartado 2291 Zona 2

Havana 10200
CUBA

---

Academia de Ciencias de Cuba
Biblioteca Nacional de Ciencia y Técnica

| | |
|---|---|
| Acta Médica | |
| | 27151657 |
| Revista Cubana de Alimentación y Nutrición | |
| | 23968257 |
| Ciencias de la Información | |

Apartado 2291 Zona 2

10200 Havana
CUBA

---

Academia de Ciencias de Cuba
Biblioteca Nacional de Ciencia y Técnica

| | |
|---|---|
| Actualidades de la Informacion Científica y Técnica | 2243882 |
| Revista Información Cient.Tecnicos series: Agropecuaria | |
| Ciencias Biológicas | |
| | 4691965 |
| Revista Cubana de Biomédicina | |

Apartado 2291 Zona 2

10200 Havana
CUBA

Academia de Ciencias de Cuba
Inst.de Investig. Fundamentales en
 Agricultura Tropical

| Calle 1, Esq 2, Santiago de Las Vegas |
| Havana |
| CUBA |

| Ciencias de la Agricultura | |
| | 4578309 |

Academia de Ciencias de Cuba
 Instituto de Ecologia y Sistematica,Biblioteca

| Carretera de Varona, Km.3 1/2 |
| Capdevila, Boyeros |
| 10800 Havana 8 |
| CUBA |

| Miscelanea Zoológica | |
| | 2242966 |
| Poeyana | |
| | 26235732 |
| Reporte de Investigación del Instituto | |
| | 19090758 |

Academia de Ciencias de Cuba
Instituto de Filosofía

| Calzada 251, Esq. a J     Vedado |
| Havana 4 |
| CUBA |

| Revista Cubana de Ciencias Sociales | |
| | 10463651 |

Academia de Ciencias de Cuba
Instituto de Meteorología

| Loma de Casa Blanca, Regla |
| Havana |
| CUBA |

| Revista Cubana de Meteorología | |
| | 22095340 |
| Reporte de Investigaciones | |
| Ciencias de la Tierra y del Espacio | |
| | 7556538 |

| INSTITUTION AND ADDRESS | PUBLICATIONS AND OCLC NO. |
|---|---|

**Ballet Nacional de Cuba**
Cuba en el Ballet, Redacción y Admin.

Calzada 509, entre D y E

Havana 4
CUBA

| Cuba en el Ballet | |
|---|---|
| | 3143142 |

**Biblioteca Nacional José Martí**
Departmento de Selección y Canje

Plaza de la Revolución

Havana
CUBA

| Cine Cubano | |
|---|---|
| | 2259400 |
| Deporte | |
| | 2454704 |
| Prisma | |
| | 19057263 |
| Bohemia | 2256648 |

**Biblioteca Nacional José Martí**
Dpto. de Selección y Canje

Plaza de la Revolución

Havana
CUBA

| Boletín Unión | |
|---|---|
| | 1473283 |
| Revista Cubana de Ciencia Avícola | |
| | 978828 |
| Revista Cubana de Derecho | |
| | 1791480 |
| Palante | 14040042 |

**Biblioteca Nacional José Martí**
Dpto. de Selección y Canje

Plaza de la Revolución

Havana
CUBA

| Cuba Internacional | |
|---|---|
| | 29652701 |
| PEL (Panorama Económico Latinoamericano) | |
| | 19760620 |
| Cuba Económica | |
| | 25968378 |
| Mujeres | 2264458 |

| INSTITUTION AND ADDRESS | PUBLICATIONS AND OCLC NO. |
|---|---|
| Biblioteca Nacional José Martí<br>Dpto. de Selección y Canje<br><br>Plaza de la Revolución<br><br>Havana<br>CUBA | Juventud Rebelde<br><br>Trabajadores<br>5980988<br><br> |
| Biblioteca Nacional José Martí<br>Dpto. de Selección y Canje<br><br>Plaza de la Revolución<br><br>Havana<br>CUBA | Revolución y Cultura<br>25199932<br>ATAC<br>2951268<br>Bibliografía Cubana<br>1519737 |
| Casa de las Américas<br>Selección y Canje<br><br>G y 3ª.<br><br>Vedado, Havana<br>CUBA | Anales del Caribe<br>11002644<br>Conjunto<br>2623241<br>Revista Casa de las Américas<br>27230617<br>Granma Resumen Semanal |
| Casa de las Américas<br>Selección y Canje<br><br>G y 3ª.<br><br>Vedado, Havana<br>CUBA | Tricontinental<br>5285397<br>Bohemia<br>2256648<br><br> |

| Institution and Address | Publications and OCLC No. | |
|---|---|---|
| Casa del Caribe<br><br>Calle 13, Nº 154, esq. a 8<br>Rpto.Vista Alegre ZP4 Apdo. Postal 4042<br>Santiago de Cuba<br>CUBA | Del Caribe | 10227611 |
| | Sierra Maestra | 28879400 |
| | | |
| | | |
| Centro Cultural "Juan Marinello"<br>Sección de Información y Canje<br><br>Oficios 420 es. Acosta<br><br>Havana 1<br>CUBA | Temas, Estudios de la Cultura | |
| | Letras Cubanas | 17367662 |
| | Revolución y Cultura | 12096488 |
| | El Caiman Barbudo    2258852 | |
| Centro Cultural "Juan Marinello"<br>Sección de Información y Canje<br><br>Oficios 420 es. Acosta<br><br>Havana 1<br>CUBA | Unión | 26238787 |
| | | |
| | | |
| | | |
| Centro de Documentacion IIIa<br>Exchange Division<br><br>Carretera Guatão km 3 1/2<br>La Lisa<br>Havana<br>CUBA | Ciencia y Tecnologia de Alimentos | 30119605 |
| | | |
| | | |
| | | |

| INSTITUTION AND ADDRESS | PUBLICATIONS AND OCLC NO. |
|---|---|

Centro de Estudios de Historia
y Org. de la Ciencia "Carlos J.Finlay"

Cuba Nº. 460
Apartado 70
Havana 1
CUBA

| Anuario | |
|---|---|
| | 22622444 |

| Reporte de Investigaciones | |
|---|---|
| | |

Centro de Estudios sobre América
Sección de Información Científica

Calle 18 Nº 316 e / 3a y 5ta
Miramar, Playa ZP 13
Havana
CUBA

| Cuadernos de Nuestra América | |
|---|---|
| | 12169552 |

Centro de Información de la Construcción
Depto. de Canje Internacional

Apartado 202

Havana 1
CUBA

| Información senal | |
|---|---|
| | |

Centro de Investigación Forestal
Centro de Documentación

Calle 174, Nº 1723 e/17B y 17C
Siboney, Zona Postal 12100
Havana
CUBA

| Revista Forestal Baracoa | |
|---|---|
| | 12630259 |

| INSTITUTION AND ADDRESS | PUBLICATIONS AND OCLC NO. |
|---|---|
| Centro de Investigaciones y Desarrollo del Petroleo<br><br>Oficio No. 154 e/Tte. Rey y Amargura<br><br>Havana 1<br>CUBA | Serie Geología 20822159 |
| Centro de Tecnología y Calidad Dpto. de Info. Científico-Técnica<br><br>Reina Nº 410 e/ Gervasio y Escobar<br><br>Havana 10200<br>CUBA | Técnica Popular 19109627 |
| Centro Meterológico Territorial<br><br>Carretera al Valle de Mayobe<br><br>Holguín CP 80500<br>CUBA | Diéresis 30581845 |
| Centro Nacional de Información de Ciencias Médicas (MINSAP)<br><br>Apartado Postal 6520<br>Calle E No. 454, Vedado<br>Havana<br>CUBA | Revista Cubana de Salud Pública 19277497<br>Revista Cubana de Investigaciones Biomédicas 17799891<br>Revista Cubana de Higiene y Epidemiología 2082867<br>Revista Cubana de Farmacia 2017361 |

| Institution and Address | Publications and OCLC No. |
|---|---|
| Centro Nacional de Investigaciones Científicas I.C.T., Canje<br><br>Apdo. 6880<br><br>Havana<br>CUBA | Revista CENIC, Ciencias Químicas    19745149<br>Resúmenes    11564765<br>Revista CENIC, Ciencias Biológicas    18694665 |
| Cinemateca de Cuba<br><br>Calle 23, 1155<br><br>Vedado, Havana 4<br>CUBA | Cine Cubano    2259400 |
| Comité Estatal de Estadísticas<br>Centro de Información Científica-Técnica<br><br>Gaveta Postal 6010<br>Almendares 156 esq. a Desagüe<br>Havana<br>CUBA | Cuba en Cifras    9191810<br>Cuba, Half yearly Economic Report    27403900 |
| Comité Estatal de Estadísticas<br>Centro de Información Científico- Técnica<br><br>Gaveta Postal 6016<br>Almendares 156 esq. a Desagüe<br>Havana<br>CUBA | Anuario Estadístico de Cuba    1168701<br>Encuesta Nacional de Fecundidad<br>Boletín Estadístico de Cuba    14253981<br>Estadística |

16

| INSTITUTION AND ADDRESS | PUBLICATIONS AND OCLC NO. |
|---|---|

Cto.de Inform.y Documentación Agropecuaria
Biblioteca - Exchange Division

| Gaveta Postal 4149 |
| --- |
| Havana |
| CUBA |

| Revista Cubana de Reprodución Animal | |
| --- | --- |
| | 10035899 |

Cto de Investigaciones de la Economía
Mundial (CIEM),Cto de Documentación

| Calle 22, No. 309 e/ 3 y 5 |
| --- |
| Playa, Havana |
| CUBA |

| Estudios sobre Estados Unidos | |
| --- | --- |
| | 18592801 |
| Temas de Economía Mundial | |
| | 13302198 |

Instituto Cubano de Investigaciones
    Derivados de la Caña Azúcar

| Apartado 4026 |
| --- |
| Havana |
| CUBA |

| Sobre los derivados de la Caña de Azúcar | |
| --- | --- |
| | 11303990 |

Instituto de Investigaciones Avícolas
Biblioteca

| Gaveta Postal no.1 |
| --- |
| Santiago de la Vegas |
| 17200 Havana |
| CUBA |

| Revista Avicultura | |
| --- | --- |
| | 2569555 |
| Revista Cubana de Ciencia Avícola | |
| 978828 | |

| INSTITUTION AND ADDRESS | PUBLICATIONS AND OCLC NO. |
|---|---|

Instituto de Investigaciones Fundamentales
en Agricultura Tropical "Alejandro Humboldt"

| Calle 2 Santiago de las Vegas |
| |
| Havana |
| CUBA |

| Reporte de Investigación INIFAT | |
| | 9842636 |
| Ciencias de la Agricultura | |
| | 4578309 |
| | |
| | |
| | |

Instituto de Literatura y Linguística
Biblioteca

| Ave. Salvador Allende 710 |
| |
| 10300 Havana |
| CUBA |

| Anuario L/L. Serie: Estudios Linguísticos | |
| | 18721879 |
| Anuario L/L. Serie: Estudios Literarios | |
| | 18721971 |
| | |
| | |
| | |

Instituto de Oceanología
Depto de Información Científico Técnica

| Calle 1ª, No. 18406, e/184 y 186 |
| |
| Playa, Havana |
| CUBA |

| Ciencias de la Tierra y del Espacio | |
| | 7556538 |
| Reporte de Investigaciones | |
| | |
| | |
| | |
| | |

Instituto Nacional de Ciencias Agrícolas
Biblioteca- Selección y Adquisición

| Gaveta Postal No. 1,San José de Las Lajas, |
| Carr.Tapaste San José Km 3 1/2 |
| 32700 Havana |
| CUBA |

| Cultivos Tropicales : CT | |
| | 10353405 |
| | |
| | |
| | |
| | |

| INSTITUTION AND ADDRESS | PUBLICATIONS AND OCLC NO. |
|---|---|

Instituto Superior Agroindustrial
Dirección de Información Científico-Técnica

Km. 3 1/2 Carretera Vía Blanca

Matanzas
CUBA

Girón
8538381

Instituto Superior de Ciencias Agropecuária
Dir. de Información Científico Técnica

Carr. Mzilo. km 17, Apdo 21

Bayamo -- Granma
CUBA

Investigación Operacional
5774702

Instituto Superior Minero Metalúrgico de Moa
C.I.C.T., Selección y Adquisición

Las Coloradas

Moa, Holguín
CUBA

Revista Minería y Geología
10736278

Instituto Superior Pedagógico Enrique
José Varona, Cto. de Documentación

Calle 108 n. 29E08   Marianao

Havana
CUBA

Verona

Cuba Socialista
8560375

Estudios Sociales

| INSTITUTION AND ADDRESS | PUBLICATIONS AND OCLC NO. |
|---|---|

Instituto Superior Politécnico
"José Antonio Echeverría" CICT

Calle 127 s/n Cujae, Marianao ZP 15

Havana
CUBA

| Ingeniería Industrial | |
|---|---|
| | 8334590 |

| Ingeniería Electrónica Automática y | |
|---|---|
| Comunicaciones | 7544069 |

| Arquitectura y Urbanismo | |
|---|---|
| | 9506930 |

| Ingeniería Energética | |
|---|---|

Instituto Superior Técnico de Holguín
CICT Selección, Adq. y Canje

Gaceta Postal No. 57
Av. 20 Aniversario
Reparto Nuevo Holguín 80400
CUBA

| Ambito | |
|---|---|
| | 29224094 |

| Diéresis | |
|---|---|
| | 30581845 |

Junta Central de Planificación
Centro de Información Científico-Técnica

20 de Mayo y Ayestarán, Plaza de

Havana
CUBA

| Revista Cuba Económica | |
|---|---|
| | 25968378 |

| Cuba, Economía Planificada | |
|---|---|
| | 14815434 |

Militante Comunista
Comité Central, Partido Comunista de Cuba

Plaza de la Revolución

Havana
CUBA

| Militante Comunista | |
|---|---|
| | 18527025 |

| INSTITUTION AND ADDRESS | PUBLICATIONS AND OCLC NO. |
|---|---|

Ministerio de Educación, Centro Nacional
de Docum. e Información Pedagógica

Obispo 160

Havana 1
CUBA

| Pedagogía Cubana | |
|---|---|
| | 22877124 |
| Educación | |
| | 1619417 |
| Revista Simientes | |
| | 10738584 |
| Ciencias Pedagógicas | |

Ministerio de la Industria Básica
Cto Nacional de Inform. Científico Técnica

Av. Salvador Allende 666

Havana
CUBA

| Revista Tecnológica | |
|---|---|
| | 4011135 |
| Boletin Técnico | |
| | |

Ministerio de la Industría Pesquera
Dpto. Información y Documentación
Científico-Técnica, Canje

Barlovento, Santa Fé, Playa C

Havana
CUBA

| Revista Cubana de Investigaciones | |
|---|---|
| Pesqueras | 5347084 |

Ministerio de Relaciones Exteriores
Dirección de Documentación

5ta. y G., Vedado

Havana
CUBA

| Bohemia | |
|---|---|
| | 2256648 |
| Cuba | |
| | 2259979 |
| Política Internacional | |
| | 1716360 |

Ministerio de Salud Pública
Hospital Psiquiátrico de la Habana

Av. de Independencia n.26520

Havana
CUBA

| Revista del Hospital Psiquiátrico de Habana | |
| --- | --- |
| | 2628430 |
| Boletin de Psicología | |
| | 7371503 |

---

Oficina Regional de Cultura para América
 Latina y El Caribe, Centro de Documentación

Calzada No. 551, Esq A D
Apartado Postal 4158, Vedado
Havana
CUBA

| Oralidad | |
| --- | --- |
| | 20686474 |

---

Organización Continental Latino
 Americana de Estudiantes

Calle 36 No. 710, 6/7a y 17

Miramar, Havana
CUBA

| OCLAE | |
| --- | --- |
| | 2674592 |

---

Revista Cuba Azúcar
Sección Canje

Apartado 6565

Havana
CUBA

| Cuba Azúcar | |
| --- | --- |
| | 2259982 |

| INSTITUTION AND ADDRESS | PUBLICATIONS AND OCLC NO. |
|---|---|
| Revista Cubana de Derecho<br>Unión Nacional de Juristas de Cuba<br><br>Calle 21 Nº 552 esq. a D    Vedado<br><br>Havana 4, CP 10400<br>CUBA | Revista Cubana de Derecho<br>1791480 |
| Revista de Letras y Artes "Ambito"<br><br>Apartado 316<br><br>Holguín, CP 80100<br>CUBA | Ambito<br>29224094 |
| Temas, Estudios de la Cultura<br><br>Apartado Postal 4169<br><br>Vedado, Havana<br>CUBA | Temas, Estudios de Cultura<br>13067983 |
| UNESCO.Oficina Regional de Cultura para<br>America Latina y El Caribe<br><br>Calzado 551 Esq. D    Vedado<br>Apartado 4158<br>Havana<br>CUBA | Informaciones Trimestrales<br>19969251 |

| INSTITUTION AND ADDRESS | PUBLICATIONS AND OCLC NO. |
|---|---|

Unión de Geología
C.N.I.G. - Biblioteca

Vía Blanca s/n e/ Carr. Central y
 Linea del Ferrocarril
Havana 11000
CUBA

| Serie Geológica | |
|---|---|
| | 11085822 |

---

Unión Escritores y Artistas de Cuba, UNEAC
Dirección de Relaciones Públicas

Calle 17 No. 351 esq. H

Vedado, Havana
CUBA

| Gaceta de Cuba | |
|---|---|
| | 15715443 |
| Unión | |
| | 26238787 |
| Revista de Literatura Cubana | |
| | 9634896 |

---

Universidad Central de las Villas
Centro de Información Científica y Tecnología

Carretera a Camajuani km. 5 1/2

Santa Clara V.C. 54830
CUBA

| Centro Agrícola | |
|---|---|
| | 3057709 |

---

Universidad Central de las Villas
Cto de Información Científica y Tecnología

Carretera a Camajuani km. 5 1/2

Santa Clara V.C. - 54830
CUBA

| Islas | |
|---|---|
| | 4766836 |
| Construcción de Maquinaria | |
| | 13292655 |
| Centro Azúcar | |
| | 7124398 |
| Arquitectura/Cuba | 2444992 |

| INSTITUTION AND ADDRESS | PUBLICATIONS AND OCLC NO. |
|---|---|

Universidad Central "Maria Abreu"
Depto. de Investigaciones Folklóricas

Santa Clara, las Villas

CUBA

| Islas | |
|---|---|
| | 4766836 |

---

Universidad de la Habana
Dir. de Información Científica y Técnica
Dpto. de Sel. y Canje

San Lazaro y L   Vedado

Havana 4
CUBA

| Educación Superior Contemporánea | |
|---|---|
| | 3522948 |
| Revista del Jardín Botánico Nacional | |
| | 7980930 |
| Universidad de La Habana | |
| | 1576210 |
| Ciencias Matemáticas   8125640 | |

---

Universidad de la Habana
Dir. de Información Científica  y Técnica
Dpto. Sel.  y Canje

San Lazaro y L

Havana 4
CUBA

| Revista Cubana de Física | |
|---|---|
| | 8125427 |
| Revista de Investigaciones Marinas | |
| | 7557742 |
| Revista Investigación Operacional | |
| | 13163728 |
| Economía y Desarrollo   1631477 | |

---

Universidad de la Habana
Dir. de Información Científica  y Técnica
Dpto. Sel.  y Canje

San Lazaro y L

Havana 4
CUBA

| Revista Cubana  de Psicologia | |
|---|---|
| | 18321016 |
| Revista Cubana de Ciencias Sociales | |
| | 10463651 |
| Revista Cubana de Educación Superior | |
| | 7557875 |

Universidad de Oriente
Biblioteca, Sección de Canje

Santiago
CUBA

| Revista Cubana de Química | |
|---|---|
| | 14758046 |
| Santiago | |
| | 2267452 |
| | |
| | |
| | |

---

House of the Assembly
Clerk's Office

Government Headquarters

Roseau
DOMINICA

| Official Gazette | |
|---|---|
| | 1670671 |
| | |
| | |
| | |
| | |

---

National Commercial Bank of Dominica

Hillsborough St.

Roseau
DOMINICA

| Annual Report and Statement of Accounts | |
|---|---|
| for the Year Ended 30th | 20785212 |
| | |
| | |
| | |
| | |

---

National Documentation Centre
Government Headquarters

Kennedy Ave.

Roseau
DOMINICA

| Annual External Trade Report (Summary | |
|---|---|
| Tables) | 29770873 |
| Travel Report for ....Quarter | |
| | |
| Demographic Statistics | |
| | |
| Annual Labour Report | |

## INSTITUTION AND ADDRESS

## PUBLICATIONS AND OCLC NO.

National Documentation Centre
Government Headquarters

Kennedy Ave.

Roseau
DOMINICA

| Report of the Public Service Commission | |
|---|---|
| for the Year Ending 31st | 18216414 |
| Budget Address | |
| | 10712697 |

---

Asociación Dominicana
  Pro Bienestar de la Familia, Inc.

Socorro Sánchez 64, Zona 1
Apartado Postal 1053
Santo Domingo
DOMINICAN REPUBLIC

| Resumenes sobre Población Dominicana | |
|---|---|
| | 1295299 |

---

Asociación Dominicana de Bibliotecarios
c/o: Biblioteca Nacional

Calle César Nicolás Penson

Santo Domingo
Dominican Republic

| Papiro | |
|---|---|
| | 5279734 |

---

Banco Central de la República Dominicana
Biblioteca

Av. Pedro Henríquez Ureña

Santo Domingo
DOMINICAN REPUBLIC

| Boletín Mensual | |
|---|---|

| INSTITUTION AND ADDRESS | PUBLICATIONS AND OCLC NO. |
|---|---|
| Biblioteca V Centenario Casa de los Jesuitas<br><br>Apto. de Correos 2664<br><br>Santo Domingo<br>DOMINICAN REPUBLIC | Quinto Centenario<br>20572252 |
| Cámara Oficial de Comercio, Agricultura Nacional<br><br>Arz. Nouel 52<br><br>Santo Domingo<br>DOMINICAN REPUBLIC | Comercio y Producción<br>1534286 |
| Estudios Sociales<br><br>Apartado 1004<br><br>Santo Domingo<br>DOMINICAN REPUBLIC | Estudios Sociales |
| Instituto Tecnológico de Santo Domingo Biblioteca<br><br>Avenida de los Próceres, Galá<br>Apdo. 249, Zona 2<br>Santo Domingo<br>DOMINICAN REPUBLIC | Boletín de Adquisiciones<br>5322766<br>Ciencia y Sociedad<br>4310107<br>INTEC Hacia el Futuro<br>4306647<br>Documentos/INTEC |

| INSTITUTION AND ADDRESS | PUBLICATIONS AND OCLC NO. |
|---|---|

**Museo del Hombre Dominicano**

Calle Pedro Henríquez Ureña
Plaza de la Cultura
Santo Domingo
DOMINICAN REPUBLIC

| Museo del Hombre Dominicano.Boletin | |
|---|---|
| | 29680208 |

---

**Revista Política: Teoría y Acción**

Av. Lope de Vega Nº 276

Santo Domingo
DOMINICAN REPUBLIC

| Política: Teoría y Acción | |
|---|---|
| | 4459470 |

---

**Univ. Nacional Pedro Henríquez Ureña**
**Biblioteca- Unidad de Selec., Adq. y Canje**

Apartado Aereo 1423

Santo Domingo
DOMINICAN REPUBLIC

| Aula | |
|---|---|
| | 1785659 |
| Biblio-notas | |
| | 5035871 |
| Cuadernos de filosofía | |
| | 14226816 |
| Cuadernos Jurídicos   4338393 | |

---

**Universidad APEC**
**Centro de Documentación**

Av. Máximo Gómez Nº 72
Apartado Postal Nº 59-2
Santo Domingo
DOMINICAN REPUBLIC

| Coloquios Jurídicos | |
|---|---|
| | 18649164 |

| INSTITUTION AND ADDRESS | PUBLICATIONS AND OCLC NO. |
|---|---|

**Universidad Autónoma de Santo Domingo**
**Biblioteca - Sección de Canje**

Apartado 1355 - Ciudad Universitaria

Santo Domingo
DOMINICAN REPUBLIC

| Boletín de Adquisiciones | |
|---|---|
| | 8545788 |

**Universidad Autónoma de Santo Domingo**
**Centro de Documentación en Salud**

Antiguo Hospital "Marion"
Zona universitaria
Santo Domingo
DOMINICAN REPUBLIC

| Archivos Dominicanos de Pediatría | |
|---|---|
| | 6336802 |

**Universidad Católica Madre y**
**Maestra**

Autopista Duarte, km. 1 1/2

Santo de los Caballeros
DOMINICAN REPUBLIC

| Eme Eme | |
|---|---|
| | 1786337 |
| Revista de Ciencias Jurídicas | |
| | 10082860 |

**Grenada Bourd of tourism**

St. George's
GRENADA

| Tropical Currents | |
|---|---|
| Statistical Review | |
| | 30498278 |

| INSTITUTION AND ADDRESS | PUBLICATIONS AND OCLC NO. |
|---|---|

Grenada Public Library

| Government Gazette | |
|---|---|
| | 1508738 |

The Carenage

St. George's
GRENADA

Institut National de la Statistique et des
  Etudes Economiques
Direction Inter-Régionale Antilles Guyane

| Tableaux économiques régionaux | |
|---|---|
| Guadeloupe | 20680076 |

Boite Postale 863 need cap on o

97175 Pointe-à-Pitre Cédex, France
GUADELOUPE

Societe d'Histoire de la Guadeloupe

| Bulletin de la Societe d'Histoire | |
|---|---|
| de la Guadeloupe | 5745643 |

Boite Postale 74

97102 Basse-Terre
GUADELOUPE

Bank of Guyana
Library

| Caribbean News Reviews | |
|---|---|
| | 15952178 |
| Annual Report and Statement of Accounts | |
| | 27345405 |
| Statistical Bulletin | |
| | 5010479 |

P.O. Box 1003

Georgetown
GUYANA

Bank of Guyana
Library

P.O. Box 1003

Georgetown
GUYANA

| International Financial & Econ. Developments | |
|---|---|
| | 24202630 |

Caribbean Community Secretariat
 Chief, Information and Documentation

Bank of Guyana Bldg.  P.O. Box 10827

Georgetown
GUYANA

| CARICOM perspective | |
|---|---|
| | 7073809 |
| Report of the Secretary-General of the | |
| Caribbean Community | 13113913 |
| CARICOM Statistics Digest | |
| | 11748268 |

Centre Spatial Guyanais

BP 726

97387 Kourou Cédex , France
GUYANA

| Recherche et Technologie en Guyane | |
|---|---|
| | 26848388 |
| Annuaire | |

Chamber of Commerce

156 Waterloo St.

Georgetown
GUYANA

| Guyana Business | |
|---|---|
| | 1461685 |

Institut d'Emission des Dpts.
  d'Outre- Mer

8 rue Christophe Colomb
BP 16
97306 Cayenne,  France
GUYANA

| Rapport d'Activité | |
|---|---|
| | 13748335 |
| Bulletin Trimestriel, Guyane | |
| | 29381539 |

Kyk-Over-Al
c/o Guysuco

22 Church Street

Georgetown
GUYANA

| Kyk-over-Al | |
|---|---|
| | 12755014 |

National LIbrary of Guyana
Exchanges

P.O. Box 10187
61 Main Street
Georgetown
GUYANA

| Guyanese National Bibliography | |
|---|---|
| | 1462419 |

University of Guyana
Library - Exchanges

P.O. Box 10  1110

Georgetown
GUYANA

| University of Guyana Bulletin | |
|---|---|
| University of Guyana Newsletter | |

Walter Roth Museum of Anthropology

| Archaeology and Anthropology | |
|---|---|
| | 6656514 |

P.O. Box 10187
61 Main Street
Georgetown
GUYANA

Bureau National d'Ethnologie
Section de Documentation

| Bulletin du Bureau National d'Ethnologie | |
|---|---|
| | 11951146 |

Boite Postale 915 need cap on o

Port-au-Prince
HAITI

Institut Français d'Haiti
Bibliothéque

| Conjonction | |
|---|---|
| | 3009058 |

Boite Postale 131 needs cap on o

Port-au-Prince
HAITI

Bank of Jamaica
Library

| Balance of Payments of Jamaica | |
|---|---|
| | 1793530 |
| Economic Statistics | |
| | 25403800 |
| Economic Bulletin | |
| | 15345081 |
| Statistical Digest     1791783 | |

P.O. Box 621

Kingston
JAMAICA

| INSTITUTION AND ADDRESS | PUBLICATIONS AND OCLC NO. |
|---|---|
| Bustamente Institute for Public and International Affairs<br><br>11 Worthington Street<br><br>Kingston 5<br>JAMAICA | Democracy Today<br>19027661 |
| Jamaica Bauxite Institute Library, Hope Gardens<br><br>P.O. Box 355<br><br>Kingston 6<br>JAMAICA | JBI Journal<br>8560537 |
| Ministry of Agriculture Research and Development Division Library<br>P.O. Box 480<br><br>Kingston 6<br>JAMAICA | Jamaica. Ministry of Agriculture. Bulletin<br>New Series 29656389 |
| National Council on Libraries,Archives & Doc. Services, Office of the Prime Minister<br><br>1 Devon Road<br>P.O. Box 272<br>Kingston 10<br>JAMAICA | Newsletter / NACOLAIS<br>28193192 |

| INSTITUTION AND ADDRESS | PUBLICATIONS AND OCLC NO. |
|---|---|

**National Library of Jamaica**
Office of the Director

12 East Street
P.O. Box 823
Kingston
JAMAICA

| Jamaica Journal | |
|---|---|
| | 1797964 |
| | |
| | |
| | |
| | |
| | |

**Planning Institute of Jamaica**
Documentation Centre

39-43 Barbados Avenue
P.O. Box 634
Kingston 5
JAMAICA

| Economic and Social Survey , Jamaica | |
|---|---|
| | 4816324 |
| Quarterly Economic Report | |
| | 12735026 |
| | |
| | |
| | |

**Statistical Institute of Jamaica**
  Library

The Towers
25 Dominica Drive
Kingston 5
JAMAICA

| External Trade Provisional | |
|---|---|
| Consumer Price Indices New | 5304712 |
| Statistical Bulletin: Consumer Price Indices | |
| | 5304718 |
| Demographic Statistics | |
| | 1789456 |
| Statistical Bulletin: External Trade 5304712 | |

**Statistical Institute of Jamaica**
Library

The Towers
25 Dominica Drive
Kingston 5
JAMAICA

| Employment, Earnings and Hours Worked in | |
|---|---|
| Large Establishments | 21440583 |
| Statistical Review | |
| | 14268527 |
| Production Statistics | |
| | 3765756 |
| Quarterly External Trade 16795330 | |

| INSTITUTION AND ADDRESS | PUBLICATIONS AND OCLC NO. |
|---|---|
| Statistical Institute of Jamaica Library | Consumer Price Indices Annual Review    1789457 |
| The Towers 25 Dominica Drive Kingston 5 JAMAICA | Statistical Yearbook of Jamaica    1795189 |
| | Statistical Abstract    14185516 |
| | Labour Force    1784568 |
| Statistical Institute of Jamaica Library | Pocketbook of Statistics    6468928 |
| The Towers 25 Dominica Drive Kingston 5 JAMAICA | National Income and Product Preliminary Report    18584110 |
| Sugar Industry Research Institute Agricultural Division | Annual Report    7922217 |
| Kendal Road  Mandeville JAMAICA | Jamaican Assoc. of Sugar Technologists Journal    9824040 |
| | Sugar Cane    20784964 |
| Supreme Court Library | Jamaica Gazette    1782397 |
| P.O. Box 491  Kingston JAMAICA | Jamaica Gazette Supplement    14175241 |

| INSTITUTION AND ADDRESS | PUBLICATIONS AND OCLC NO. |
|---|---|
| University of the West Indies<br>Carimac<br><br>Mona, Kingston 7<br>JAMAICA | Cross Over: A Networking Newsletter — 27314292 |
| University of the West Indies<br>Institute of Econ. & Social Research, Library<br><br>Mona, Kingston 7<br>JAMAICA | Social and Economic Studies — 85977602 |
| University of the West Indies<br>Library - Gifts and Exchanges<br><br>Mona, Kingston 7<br>JAMAICA | African Studies Assoc.of West Indies Bulletin — 1661186<br>Journal of Caribbean History — 1588454<br>Journal of West Indian Literature — 15211499<br>Jamaica Library Assoc. Bulletin 6674216 |
| University of the West Indies<br>Library - Gifts and Exchanges<br><br>Mona, Kingston 7<br>JAMAICA | Vice-Chancellor's Report to Council — 15669591<br>Caribbean Quarterly — 843029<br>Report on the Libraries — 2472331<br>Departmental Reports |

| INSTITUTION AND ADDRESS | PUBLICATIONS AND OCLC NO. |
|---|---|

**University of the West Indies**
**Library - Gifts and Exchanges**

Mona, Kingston 7
JAMAICA

| Jamaican Historical Review | 1782874 |
|---|---|
| Report of the Cocoa Industry Board | 19914091 |
| Jamaican National Bibliography | 4760593 |
| Calendar | |

**Bank van de Nederlandse Antillen**
**Research Department**

Breedestratt Nr. 1

Willemstad, Curaçao
NETHERLANDS ANTILLES

| Annual Report | 18131944 |
|---|---|
| Quarterly Bulletin | 5539020 |
| Selected Monetary Figures as per the end of. | 14205372 |
| | |

**Centraal Bureau voor de Statistiek**

Fort Amsterdam

Willemstad, Curaçao
NETHERLANDS ANTILLES

| Statistical Yearbook of the Netherlands Antilles | 9998841 |
|---|---|
| Yearbook of the Imports and Exports of Curaçao and Bonaire | 24148472 |
| | |
| | |

**Centraal Historish Archief**

Scarlooweg 77

Willemstad, Curaçao
NETHERLANDS ANTILLES

| Import & Export Qrterly Statistics of Curaçao & Bonaire by Commodity | |
|---|---|
| Import & Export Qrterly Statistics of Curaçao & Bonaire by Country | |
| Lanternu | 10164189 |
| | |

| INSTITUTION AND ADDRESS | PUBLICATIONS AND OCLC NO. | |
| --- | --- | --- |
| Departamento de Recursos Naturales<br>Laboratorio de Investigaciones Pesqueras | Actualidades Pesqueras | |
| | Informe Técnico | |
| Apartado 665, Marina Station<br><br>Mayagüez,<br>PUERTO RICO 00680 | | |
| | | |
| | | |
| Universidad de Puerto Rico<br>Recinto Mayaguez, Biblioteca General, Canje | Atenea | 2937856 |
| | Caribbean Journal of Science | 1553365 |
| Mayagüez,<br>PUERTO RICO 00708 | Contribuciones | |
| | | |
| Universidad Católica de Puerto Rico<br>Bca Encarnación Valdez, Depto.de Canje | Horizontes | 1697154 |
| | | |
| Ponce,<br>PUERTO RICO 00732 | | |
| | | |
| Universidad Católica de Puerto Rico<br>Escuela de Derecho, Biblioteca | Revista de Derecho Puertorriqueño | 1763895 |
| | | |
| Ponce,<br>PUERTO RICO 00732 | | |
| | | |

| INSTITUTION AND ADDRESS | PUBLICATIONS AND OCLC NO. |
|---|---|

**Tribunal Supremo de Puerto Rico**
**Biblioteca**

P.O. Box 2392

San Juan,
PUERTO RICO   00903

| | |
|---|---|
| Official Translations of the Opinions of the Supreme Court of Puerto Rico | 9401638 |

**Centro de Estudios Avanzados de**
**Puerto Rico**

Apartado S-4467

San Juan
PUERTO RICO   00904

| | |
|---|---|
| Revista del Centro de Estudios Avanzados de Puerto Rico | 15715472 |

**Instituto de Cultura Puertorriqueña**
**Of. de Canje y Distribución de Publicaciones**

Apartado 4184

San Juan,
PUERTO RICO 00905

| | |
|---|---|
| Boletín de la Académia Puertorriqueña de la Historia | 1460629 |
| Revista del Instituto de Cultura Puertorriqueña | 1933454 |

**Universidad Interamericana de P.R.**
**Facultad de Derecho**

P.O. Box 8897
Fernández Juncos Station
Santurce,
PUERTO RICO   00910

| | |
|---|---|
| Revista Jurídica de la Universidad Interamericana de Puerto Rico | 2254903 |

41

| INSTITUTION AND ADDRESS | PUBLICATIONS AND OCLC NO. |
|---|---|

**Universidad del Sagrado Corazón**
**Centro de Investigaciones  Académicas**

| Apartado 12383 / Correo Calle Loíza |
| --- |
| Santurce, |
| PUERTO RICO   00914 |

| Avances de Investigaciones | |
| --- | --- |

**Tribunal General de Justicia**
**Oficina de Administración de los Tribunales**

| Hato Rey Station, Box 917 |
| --- |
| Hato Rey, |
| PUERTO RICO   00919 |

| Informe Anual de la Rama Judicial | |
| --- | --- |
|  | 26556451 |

**Universidad Interamericana de P.R.**
**Depto. Ciencias Sociales**

| Apartado Postal 1293 |
| --- |
| Hato Rey |
| PUERTO RICO   00919 |

| Homines:Revista  de Ciencias Sociales | |
| --- | --- |
|  | 29892191 |

**Universidad de Puerto Rico**
**Biblioteca de Derecho**

| UPR Station |
| --- |
| Río Piedras, |
| PUERTO RICO   00931 |

| Revista Jurídica | |
| --- | --- |
|  | 1763967 |
| Estudios del Caribe | |

| INSTITUTION AND ADDRESS | PUBLICATIONS AND OCLC NO. |
|---|---|
| Universidad de Puerto Rico,Facultad de Humanidades, Depto. de Bellas Artes<br><br>Rio Piedras<br>PUERTO RICO 00931 | Revista de Estudios Hispánicos — 998931<br>Diálogos — 2323262 |
| Universidad de Puerto Rico<br>Sistema de Bibliotecas Sec. de Adq.-Canje<br><br>Box 23302 UPR Station<br><br>Río Piedras,<br>PUERTO RICO    00931-3302 | Plural — 17976561<br>Diálogos:Revista del Departmento de Filosofía — 2323262<br>La Torre — 1767638<br>Revista de Ciencias Sociales    1763885 |
| Universidad de Puerto Rico<br>Sistema de Bibliotecas,Sec.de Adq.-Canje<br><br>Box 23302 UPR Station<br><br>Río Piedras,<br>PUERTO RICO    00931-3302 | El Cuervo<br>Caribbean Studies — 844091 |
| Government Development Bank for Puerto Rico,  Library<br><br>P.O. Box 42001, Minillas Station<br><br>San Juan,<br>PUERTO RICO    00940 | Annual Report — 20865606<br>Puerto Rico Business Review — 4521381<br>Puerto Rico Economic Indicators — 14047970 |

| INSTITUTION AND ADDRESS | PUBLICATIONS AND OCLC NO. |
|---|---|

Junta de Planificación
Biblioteca

Apartado 41119, Minillas Station

San Juan,
PUERTO RICO    00940-99850

| Informe Económico al Gobernador | |
|---|---|
| | 4098904 |
| Estadísticas Socioeconómicas, Puerto Rico | |
| | 18769623 |

---

Nevis Public Library
Prince William Street

Charlestown, Nevis
ST. CHRISTOPHER & NEVIS

| SKNED Newsletter | |
|---|---|

---

Government Information Service
Chief Information Officer

Brazil St.
Monplaisir Bldg.
Castries
ST. LUCIA

| Weekly Focus | |
|---|---|

---

St. Lucia National Trust

P.O. Box 525
Vigie
Castries
ST. LUCIA

| Conservation News | |
|---|---|
| | 29432005 |

44

| INSTITUTION AND ADDRESS | PUBLICATIONS AND OCLC NO. |
|---|---|

**Department of Libraries and Archives**
Director of Library Services

Lower Middle St.

Kingstown, St. Vincent
ST. VINCENT AND THE GRENADINES

Unity

The Vincentian

The News

---

**Anton de Kom Universiteit van Suriname**
Centraalbibliotheek - Exchanges

Leysweg
P.O. Box 9212
Paramaribo
SURINAM

Nationale Ontwikkelingsbank
Jaarverslag/Annual Report
Staatsblad van de Republiek Suriname
6685692

---

**Centrale Bank van Suriname**

P.O. Box 1801

Paramaribo
SURINAM

Condensed Balance Sheet

Selected Monetary Figures

Verslag
1789005

---

**Stichting Surinaams Museum**

P.O. Box 2306

Paramaribo
SURINAM

Mededelingen
8587609

| Trinidad and Tobago Electricity Commission Public Relations Office | | |
|---|---|---|
| P.O. Box 121 | | |
| 63 Frederick St. | | |
| Port-of-Spain | | |
| TRINIDAD AND TOBAGO | | |

| Annual Report | |
|---|---|
| Current Affairs | |
| | 13433573 |
| Watts Happening | |
| | 19826275 |
| | |

| Trinidad and Tobago Institute of the West Indies | | |
|---|---|---|
| 24 Abercombie St. (Annexe) | | |
| Port-of-Spain | | |
| TRINIDAD AND TOBAGO | | |

| Trinidad and Tobago Review | |
|---|---|
| | 4880960 |
| | |
| | |
| | |

| Central Bank of Trinidad & Tobago Research Library | | |
|---|---|---|
| P.O Box 1250 | | |
| Port-of-Spain | | |
| TRINIDAD & TOBAGO | | |

| Annual Economic Survey | |
|---|---|
| | 17158975 |
| Quarterly Statistical Digest | |
| | 9058233 |
| Monthly Statistical Digest | |
| | 6759029 |
| Annual Report     25512008 | |

| Central Bank of Trinidad & Tobago Research Library | | |
|---|---|---|
| P.O. Box 1250 | | |
| Port-of-Spain | | |
| TRINIDAD & TOBAGO | | |

| Quarterly Economic Bulletin | |
|---|---|
| | 4282134 |
| | |
| | |
| | |
| | |

| INSTITUTION AND ADDRESS | PUBLICATIONS AND OCLC NO. |
|---|---|
| Central Statistical Office<br>Library<br><br>23 Park Street<br>P.O. Box 98<br>Port-of-Spain<br>TRINIDAD & TOBAGO | Balance of Payments of Trinidad & Tobago — 2092958<br>Annual Statistical Digest — 1157323<br>International Travel Report — 2093332<br>Report on Education Statistics  11633536 |
| Central Statistical Office<br>Library<br><br>23 Park Street<br>P.O. Box<br>Port-of-Spain<br>TRINIDAD & TOBAGO | Economic Indicators — 2243056<br>Trade Bulletin — 30387562<br>Overseas Trade — 2096468<br>Labour Force Report |
| Central Statistical Office<br>Library<br><br>23 Park Street<br>P.O. Box<br>Port-of-Spain<br>TRINIDAD & TOBAGO | Population & Vital Statistics Report — 26127888 |
| Economic Commission for Latin America<br>Office for the Caribbean<br><br>P.O. Box 1113, Salvatori Bldg. Rm 300<br><br>Port-of-Spain<br>TRINIDAD & TOBAGO | Economic Activity in Caribbean Countries — 4863649<br>CARISPLAN Abstracts — 9925691 |

**Institute of Marine Affairs**

P.O. Box 3160

Carenage
TRINIDAD & TOBAGO

| Caribbean Marine Studies | |
|---|---|
| | 27960368 |
| CCOSNET News | |
| | |
| Annual Report | |
| | |
| | |

**Ministry of Energy and Natural Resources**

4th Floor, Salvatori Bldg.
P.O. Box 96
Port-of-Spain
TRINIDAD & TOBAGO

| Annual report | |
|---|---|
| | |
| Petroleum Industry Monthly Bulletin | |
| | |
| | |
| | |
| | |

**University of the West Indies**
**Library - Gifts and Exchanges**

St. Augustine, Trinidad
TRINIDAD & TOBAGO

| Trinidad & Tobago National Bibliography | |
|---|---|
| | 2791259 |
| Tropical Agriculture;journal of the Faculty of Agriculture | |
| | |
| CARICOM Perspective | |
| | 7073809 |
| | |

## PUBLICATIONS/PUBLICACIONES/PUBLICAÇÕES

Publications may be ordered from the Secretariat.

*FINAL REPORT AND WORKING PAPERS.* Nos. 1-16, 20-21 and 23 are out of print. Nos. 17-19 (1972-74) are available from the Secretariat at $21.75 each. (Note: Vol. 3 of No. 19 contains the papers of the post-conference, the First Symposium on Spanish-Language Materials for Children and Young adults, April, 1974.)

No. 22. **The Multifaceted Role of the Latin American Subject Specialist.** 1979. $25 (plus $2.50, P&H).

No. 24. **Windward, Leeward, and Main: Caribbean Studies and Library Resources.** 1980. $35 (plus $2.50, P&H).

No. 25. **Library Resources on Latin America: New Perspectives for the 1980's.** 1981. $35. (plus $2.50, P&H).

*PAPERS* (continue *FINAL REPORT AND WORKING PAPERS)*

No. 26. **Latin American Economic Issues: Information Needs and Sources.** 1984. $45 (plus $2.50, P&H).

No. 27. **Public Policy Issues and Latin American Library Resources.** 1984. $45. (plus $2.50, P&H).

No. 28. **The Central American Connection: Library Resources and Access.** 1985. $35 (plus $2.50, P&H).

No. 29. **Collection Development: Cooperation at the National and Local Levels.** 1987. $35 (plus $2.50, P&H).

No. 30. **Latin American Masses and Minorities: Their Images and Realities.** 2 vols. 1987. $55 (plus $3.00, P&H).

No. 31. **Intellectual Migrations: The Transcultural Contributions of European and Latin American Emigrés.** 1988. $47.50 (plus $2.50, P&H).

No. 32. **Caribbean Collections: Recession Strategies for Libraries.** 1989. $47.50 (plus $2.50, P&H).

No. 33. **Frontiers, Borders and Hinterlands.** 1990. $50 (plus 2.50, P&H).

No. 34. **Artistic Representation of Latin American Diversity: Sources and Collections.** 1993. $50 (plus 2.50, P&H).

No. 35. **Continuity and Change in Brazil and the Southern Cone: Research Trends and Library Collections for the year 2000.** 1992. $50 (plus $2.50 P&H).

No. 36. **Latin American Studies into the Twenty-First Century: New Focus, New Formats, New Challenges.** 1993. $52 (plus $2.50, P&H).

No. 37. **SALALM and the Area Studies Community.** 1994. $45 (plus $2.50, P&H).

*BIBLIOGRAPHY SERIES*

No. 2. Woodbridge, Hensley, Ed. **A Basic List of Latin American Materials in Spanish, Portuguese, and French.** 1975. $10 (plus $2, P&H).

No. 3. Fernández-Caballero, Carlos. F.S. **Paraguái tai hume, tove Paraguái arandu taisarambi ko yvy apére: The Paraguayan Bibliography.** Vol. 2. $10 (plus $1.50, P&H).

No. 4. Lo, Sara de Mundo and Beverly Phillips. **Colombian Serial Publications in the University of Illinois Library at Urbana-Champaign.** 1978. $8. (plus $2, P&H).

No. 5. Robinson, Barbara J. **Doctoral Dissertations in Hispanic-American Literature: A Bibliography of Dissertations Completed in the U.S., 1964-74.** 1979. $6.50 (plus $1.50, P&H).

No. 6. Ballantyne, Lygia Maria F. C. **Haitian Publications: An Acquisitions Guide and Bibliography.** 1980. $10. (plus $2, P&H).

No. 7. Sonntag, Gabriela. **Eva Perón: Books, Articles, and Other Sources of Study: An Annotated Bibliography.** 1983. $6.50 (plus $2, P&H).

No. 8. Covington, Paula Hattox. **Indexed Journals: A Guide to Latin American Serials.** 1983. $20 (plus $3, P&H).

No. 9. Block, David and Howard L. Karno, Eds. **Directory of Vendors of Latin American Library Materials.** 1983. $8 (plus $2, P&H).

*BIBLIOGRAPHY AND REFERENCE SERIES* (continues *BIBLIOGRAPHY SERIES*) (Items in print)

No. 10. Loroña, Lionel, Ed. **Bibliography of Latin American Bibliographies, 1982-1983.** 1984. $8 (plus $2.50, P&H).

No. 12. Valk, Barbara G., Ed. **Index to the SALALM Papers,** 1956-1980. 1985. $6.50 to members (plus $2, P&H).

No. 13. Rovirosa, Dolores F. **Jorge Mañach: Bibliografía.** 1985. $15 (plus $3, P&H).

No. 14. Roberts, Audrey. **Bibliography of Commissions of Enquiry and Other Government-Sponsored Reports on the Commonwealth Caribbean, 1900-1975.** 1985. $15 (plus $2.50, P&H).

No. 21. Ilgen, William D. and Deborah Jakubs. **Acquistions Manual/Manual de Adquisiciones/Manual de Aquisicões.** 1988. $18 (plus $2.50, P&H). In Latin America and the Caribbean: $10 (plus $2.50, P&H).

No. 23. Lorona, Lionel, Ed. **Bibiography of Latin American and Caribbean Bibliographies, 1987-1988.** $13 (plus $2.50, P&H).

No. 24. Valk, Barbara G., Ed. **Index to the SALALM Papers, 1981.** 1985. 1989. $3 to members (plus $1.50, P&H).

No. 25. Loroña, Lionel, Ed. **Bibliography of Latin American and Caribbean Bibliographies, 1988-1989.** 1989. $15 (plus $2.50, P&H).

No. 26. Simoneau, Karin. **South American Population Censuses Since Independence: an Annotated Bibliography of Secondary Sources.** 1990. $22.50 (plus $2.50, P&H).

No. 27. Loroña, Lionel, Ed. **Bibliography of Latin American and Caribbean Bibliographies, 1989-1990.** 1990. $15 (plus $2.50, P&H).

No. 28. Muricy, Carmen M. **The Brazilian Amazon: Institutions and Publications.** 1990. $23.50 (plus $2.50, P&H).

No. 29. Miller, Shelley, Comp. **Serial Publications Available by Exchange: Mexico, Central America and Panama.** 1992. $20 (plus $2.50, P&H).

No. 30. Loroña, Lionel, Ed. **Bibliography of Latin American and Caribbean Bibliographies, 1990-1991.** $19 (plus $2.50, P&H).

No. 31. Loroña, Lionel, Ed. **Bibliography of Latin American and Caribbean Bibliographies, 1991-1992.** $17.50 (plus $2.50, P&H).

No. 32. Karno, Howard L. and Beverly Joy-Karno. **Directory of Vendors of Latin American Library Materials.** Fourth edition, revised. 1993. $17 (plus $2.50 P&H).

No. 33. De Varona, Esperanza B. **Posters of the Cuban Diaspora: A Bibliography.** 1993. $22 (plus 2.50 P&H).

No. 34. Williams, Gayle Ann, Ed. **Bibliography of Latin American and Caribbean Bibliographies, 1992-1993.** 1993. $19.50 (plus $2.50, P&H).

No. 35. Williams, Gayle Ann Ed. **Bibliography of Latin American and Caribbean Bibliographies, 1993-1994.** 1994. $23.50 (plus $2.50 P&H).

No. 36. Miller, Shelley and Gabriela Sonntag-Grigera, Comps. **Serial Publications Available by Exchange: Caribbean Area.** 1994. $17 (plus $2.50 P&H).

*OTHER PUBLICATIONS*

**Microfilming Projects Newsletter.** Vol. 1, no. 1-, 1964-, Index: 1-20. Issued annually as a working paper of the Seminar. Subscriptions available from the Secretriat at $8.50 per year.

**SALALM Newsletter.** Vol. 1, no. 1-, Jan. 1973-. Distributed without charge to members. Subscriptions available from the Secretariat at $25 per year. Back files are available at $15 per volume.

BIBLIOGRAPHY AND REFERENCE SERIES, 37

# SERIAL PUBLICATIONS AVAILABLE BY EXCHANGE

## SPANISH SOUTH AMERICA

### COMPILED AND EDITED BY GABRIELA SONNTAG

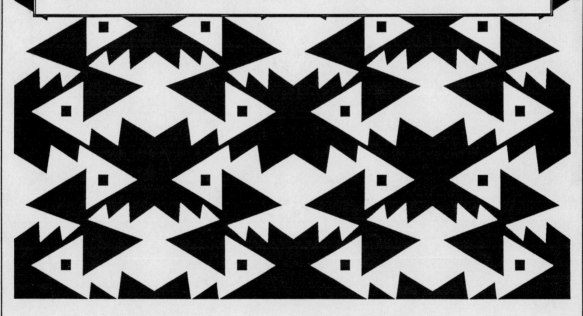

SEMINAR ON THE ACQUISITION OF
LATIN AMERICAN LIBRARY MATERIALS
General Library
University of New Mexico
Albuquerque, New Mexico USA